MACHINES CLOSE-UP

RESCUE VEHICLES

Daniel Gilpin and Alex Pang

Marshall Cavendish
Benchmark

New York

This edition first published in 2011 in the United States by
Marshall Cavendish Benchmark

An imprint of Marshall Cavendish Corporation

All rights reserved.

No part of this publication may be reproduced, stored in a retrieval system or transmitted, in any form or by any means, electronic, mechanical, photocopying, recording, or otherwise, without the prior permission of the copyright owner. Request for permission should be addressed to the Publisher, Marshall Cavendish Corporation, 99 White Plains Road, Tarrytown, NY 10591.
Tel: (914) 332-8888, fax: (914) 332-1888.

Website: www.marshallcavendish.us

This publication represents the opinions and views of the author based on Daniel Gilpin's and Alex Pang's personal experience, knowledge, and research. The information in this book serves as a general guide only. The author and publisher have used their best efforts in preparing this book and disclaim liability rising directly and indirectly from the use and application of this book.

Other Marshall Cavendish Offices:
Marshall Cavendish International (Asia) Private Limited, 1 New Industrial Road, Singapore 536196 • Marshall Cavendish International (Thailand) Co Ltd. 253 Asoke, 12th Flr, Sukhumvit 21 Road, Klongtoey Nua, Wattana, Bangkok 10110, Thailand • Marshall Cavendish (Malaysia) Sdn Bhd, Times Subang, Lot 46, Subang Hi-Tech Industrial Park, Batu Tiga, 40000 Shah Alam, Selangor Darul Ehsan, Malaysia

Marshall Cavendish is a trademark of Times Publishing Limited

Copyright © 2009 David West Children's Books

Library of Congress Cataloging-in-Publication Data

Gilpin, Daniel.
Rescue vehicles / Daniel Gilpin and Alex Pang.
p. cm.
Includes index.
Summary: "Reveals and discusses the intricate internal workings of rescue vehicles"--Provided by publisher.
ISBN 978-1-60870-111-7
1. Emergency vehicles--Juvenile literature. 2. Search and rescue aircraft--Juvenile literature. 3. Search and rescue boats--Juvenile literature. 4. Rescue work--Juvenile literature. 5. Search and rescue operations--Juvenile literature. I. Pang, Alex. II. Title.

TL235.8.G55 2011
628.9'2--dc22
2009043258

First published in 2009 by Wayland
Hachette Children's Books
338 Euston Road
London NW1 3BH
Wayland Australia
Level 17/207 Kent Street
Sydney, NSW 2000

Produced by
David West Children's Books
7 Princeton Court
55 Felsham Road
London SW15 1AZ

Editor: Katharine Pethick
Designer: Gary Jeffrey
Illustrator: Alex Pang
Consultant: Steve Parker

The photographs in this book are used by permission and through the courtesy of:
Abbreviations: t-top, m-middle, b-bottom, r-right, l-left, c-center.
4b, U.S. Army; 6l, skuds; 6b, Rozalyn Dorsay; 7tr, Library of Congress; 7ml, Wyrdlight; 7bl, gsloan; 7br, dave_7; 30t, Dtom; 8t, lifeboat rnli; 8b, Mariners Weather Log; 9t, Bmpower; 30m, Bell Helicopter; 30b, carbon motors corp

Printed in China
135642

CONTENTS

16 AIRPORT FIREFIGHTING VEHICLE

18 TOW TRUCK

20 SUBMARINE RESCUE VEHICLE

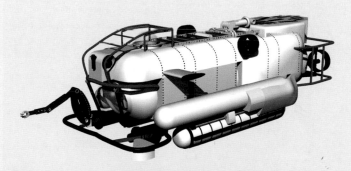

22 LIFEBOAT

24 FIREFIGHTING BOAT

26 AIR/SEA RESCUE HELICOPTER

28 AERIAL FIREFIGHTER

Glossary Words: when a word is printed in **bold**, you can look up its meaning in the Glossary on page 31.

INTRODUCTION

Rescue vehicles are a part of modern life, and their sirens are a familiar sound in our towns and cities. Many of us take them for granted and forget the important role they play. The reality is that without them the world would be a much more dangerous place in which to live.

MACHINES TO THE RESCUE
Motorized vehicles and their operators are a vital part of most emergency services, working on land, air, and sea to protect property and save people's lives.

HOW TO USE THIS BOOK

MAIN TEXT
Explains the history of the vehicle and outlines its primary role. Information, such as which services use the vehicle, is also covered here.

MAIN ILLUSTRATION
Shows the internal structure of the vehicle and gives information on the positions of its various working parts.

EQUIPMENT
Displays the specialized equipment carried by the vehicle and used by the people who operate it, in their different roles.

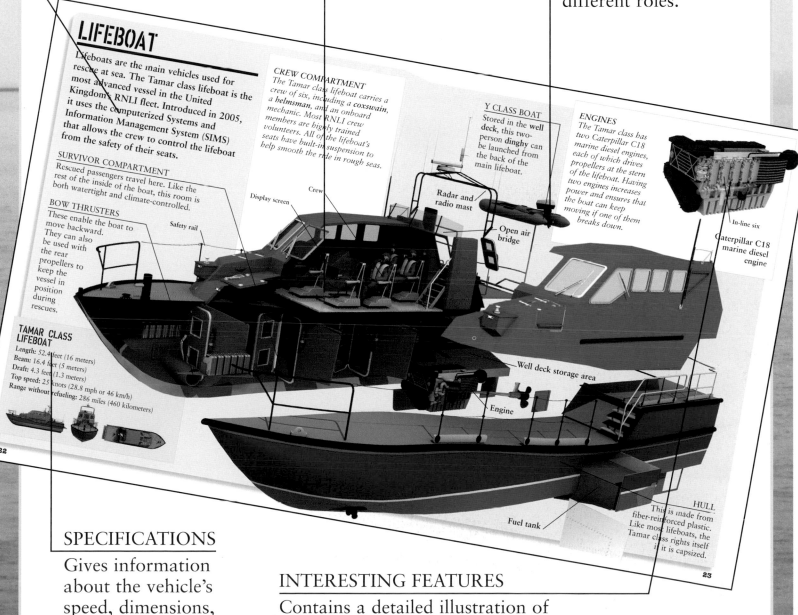

LIFEBOAT

Lifeboats are the main vehicles used for rescue at sea. The Tamar class lifeboat is the most advanced vessel in the United Kingdom's RNLI fleet. Introduced in 2005, it uses the computerized Systems and Information Management System (SIMS) that allows the crew to control the lifeboat from the safety of their seats.

SURVIVOR COMPARTMENT
Rescued passengers travel here. Like the rest of the inside of the boat, this room is both watertight and climate-controlled.

BOW THRUSTERS
These enable the boat to move backward. They can also be used with the rear propellers to keep the vessel in position during rescues.

TAMAR CLASS LIFEBOAT
Length: 52.4 feet (16 meters)
Beam: 16.4 feet (5 meters)
Draft: 4.3 feet (1.3 meters)
Top speed: 25 knots (28.8 mph or 46 km/h)
Range without refueling: 286 miles (460 kilometers)

CREW COMPARTMENT
The Tamar class lifeboat carries a crew of six, including a coxswain, a helmsman, and an onboard mechanic. Most RNLI crew members are highly trained volunteers. All of the lifeboat's seats have built-in suspension to help smooth the ride in rough seas.

Display screen

Crew

Safety rail

Y CLASS BOAT
Stored in the well deck, this two-person dinghy can be launched from the back of the main lifeboat.

Radar and radio mast

Open air bridge

ENGINES
The Tamar class has two Caterpillar C18 marine diesel engines, each of which drives propellers at the stern of the lifeboat. Having two engines increases power and ensures that the boat can keep moving if one of them breaks down.

In-line six

Caterpillar C18 marine diesel engine

Well deck storage area

Engine

Fuel tank

HULL
This is made from fiber-reinforced plastic. Like most lifeboats, the Tamar class rights itself if it is capsized.

22

23

SPECIFICATIONS
Gives information about the vehicle's speed, dimensions, and operational range.

INTERESTING FEATURES
Contains a detailed illustration of the engine or another design feature that makes the vehicle unique. Informative text explains the feature's function.

RESCUES ON LAND

The history of the rescue vehicle is a long one. Over the centuries these machines have helped to save countless people. Today they are a regular sight all around the world.

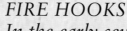

FIRE TRUCKS

Fires have always been a problem, particularly in towns and crowded cities. The earliest mechanized firefighting vehicles were developed in the nineteenth century. When the **internal combustion engine** was invented, these horse-drawn units were replaced by more modern, self-propelled fire trucks.

FIRE HOOKS
In the early seventeenth century, people used long-handled hooks to pull the straw from roofs to stop the spread of fires.

VICTORIAN STEAM PUMPER
The first fire trucks were horse-drawn pumps powered by a steam engine.

1950s LADDER FIRE TRUCK

AIRPORT CRASH FIRE TRUCK

ARFF VEHICLES

Early Aircraft Rescue and Firefighting (ARFF) vehicles were developed during World War II. This development increased as the number of airports offering commercial flights grew.

AMBULANCES

Motorized ambulances first appeared in the early twentieth century. The concept of the ambulance was well established because horse-drawn **municipal ambulances** were already in use. Early motorized ambulances were little more than covered trucks, but in time the equipment they carried became more sophisticated.

MODEL T FORD AMBULANCE

MILITARY AMBULANCE
Before there were motorized ambulances, people used horses and carts. The military created the first organized ambulance services.

1970s CADILLAC AMBULANCE

PATROL CARS

The invention of the patrol car allowed police officers to cover larger areas. By the 1940s, patrol cars were in widespread use in the United States. Soon, other nations' forces began using them in ever greater numbers.

1940s "BLACK AND WHITE"

1930s FORD WRECKER

TOW TRUCKS

Tow trucks developed as cars became more common. Since broken-down cars could not always be fixed on the road, specialized vehicles would tow damaged cars away.

AIR AND WATER

The business of saving lives is not confined to land. Boats and aircraft are also used to fight fires and rescue people. These vehicles are often highly specialized.

RNLI LIFEBOAT 1936
The men and women of the United Kingdom's RNLI have saved many thousands of lives. The organization is a charity run largely by volunteers. Since 1980, it has rescued an average of twenty-two people a day.

SEARCH AND RESCUE AT SEA

The history of lifeboats dates back several centuries. The earliest vessels were simple rowing boats, operated by coastal people to help sailors in trouble. The oldest lifeboat organization is the United Kingdom's Royal National Lifeboat Institution (RNLI), founded in 1824.

U.S. COAST GUARD RESCUE BOAT
The U.S. Coast Guard combines its main role of monitoring the movement of ships with carrying out rescues at sea.

AIR SEARCH AND RESCUE

Aircraft also play a part in rescues at sea. Helicopters have been used in this role for more than fifty years. Air search and rescue missions also take place on land, rescuing stranded climbers from cliffs or mountains, for example.

HELICOPTER RESCUE

AERIAL FIREFIGHTING

FIREFIGHTING FROM AIR AND SEA

Fireboats were designed to tackle blazes on ships, although they can also fight fires in dockside buildings. Aerial firefighting machines, such as water bombers, put out fires in forests or in places inaccessible to land-based units.

FIREBOAT
Refurbished vintage vessels like the Edward M. Cotter, *built in 1900, are still used as working fireboats.*

SUBMARINE RESCUE

Today there are even vehicles that can rescue people underwater. Submarine rescue vehicles are rare, but so are the accidents that need them. These vehicles and crews often travel long distances to undertake rescue missions.

DEEP SEA RESCUE VEHICLE 2 AVALON

U.S. PATROL CAR

The police are often the first to be called to an accident. Different countries' police forces use different vehicles, but in the United States, the Ford Crown Victoria is the most widely used car of all. This model is also sold to the general public, but the police version has several adaptations.

BODYWORK AND CHASSIS

The Ford Crown Victoria has body-on-frame construction. Having a separate body on a rigid frame makes the vehicle easier to repair after minor accidents, because the chassis does not get damaged. Additions made to police cars include sirens and emergency lights.

Shotgun

Assault rifle

WEAPONS RACK
Most U.S. police officers carry a shotgun or patrol rifle in the front of the car. It is usually stowed in a weapons rack, either between the seats or near the dashboard so that it is easily accessible but not in the way.

Cylinders

Gearbox

Ford V8 gas engine

Radiator

ENGINE
The Ford Crown Victoria has a 250 horsepower V8 engine, which gives it impressive acceleration when needed. The car is rear-wheel drive and has a four-speed automatic transmission.

Chassis

Laptop computer

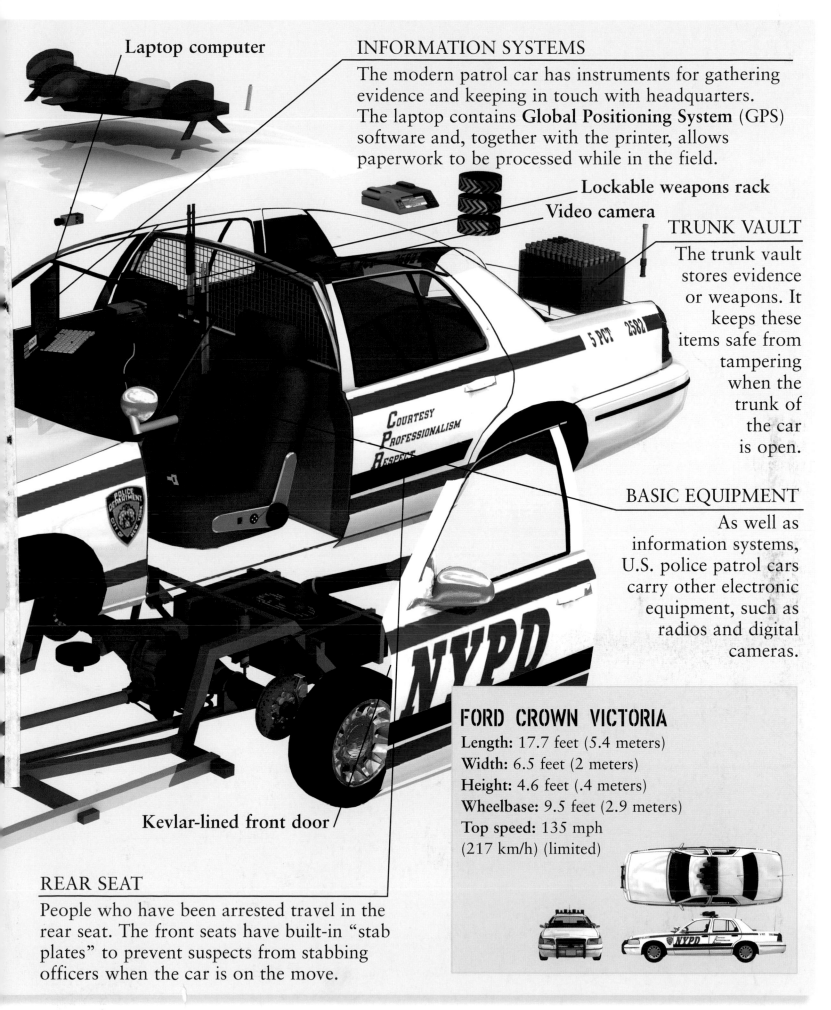

INFORMATION SYSTEMS

The modern patrol car has instruments for gathering evidence and keeping in touch with headquarters. The laptop contains **Global Positioning System** (GPS) software and, together with the printer, allows paperwork to be processed while in the field.

Lockable weapons rack

Video camera

TRUNK VAULT

The trunk vault stores evidence or weapons. It keeps these items safe from tampering when the trunk of the car is open.

BASIC EQUIPMENT

As well as information systems, U.S. police patrol cars carry other electronic equipment, such as radios and digital cameras.

Kevlar-lined front door

FORD CROWN VICTORIA

Length: 17.7 feet (5.4 meters)
Width: 6.5 feet (2 meters)
Height: 4.6 feet (.4 meters)
Wheelbase: 9.5 feet (2.9 meters)
Top speed: 135 mph (217 km/h) (limited)

REAR SEAT

People who have been arrested travel in the rear seat. The front seats have built-in "stab plates" to prevent suspects from stabbing officers when the car is on the move.

AMBULANCE

An ambulance transports patients to the hospital as quickly as possible. The latest ambulances carry sophisticated equipment that saves even more lives by offering treatment inside, before reaching the hospital. The Ford E-350 contains all the most commonly needed equipment to keep patients alive during their trip.

EMERGENCY EQUIPMENT

*Ambulance crews are prepared for all kinds of medical emergencies and the ambulances carry a wide range of equipment. Ambulances usually have a stretcher—a simple bed for carrying patients to and from the vehicle and supporting their bodies inside it. Other more high-tech equipment includes oxygen masks for helping patients with their breathing and **defibrillators** for restarting the heart.*

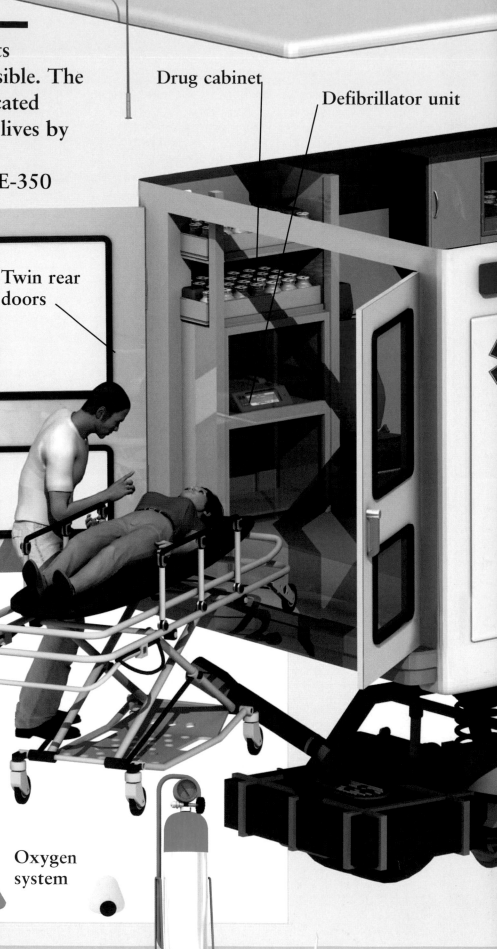

Drug cabinet

Defibrillator unit

Twin rear doors

Stretcher

Oxygen system

Defibrillator/monitor

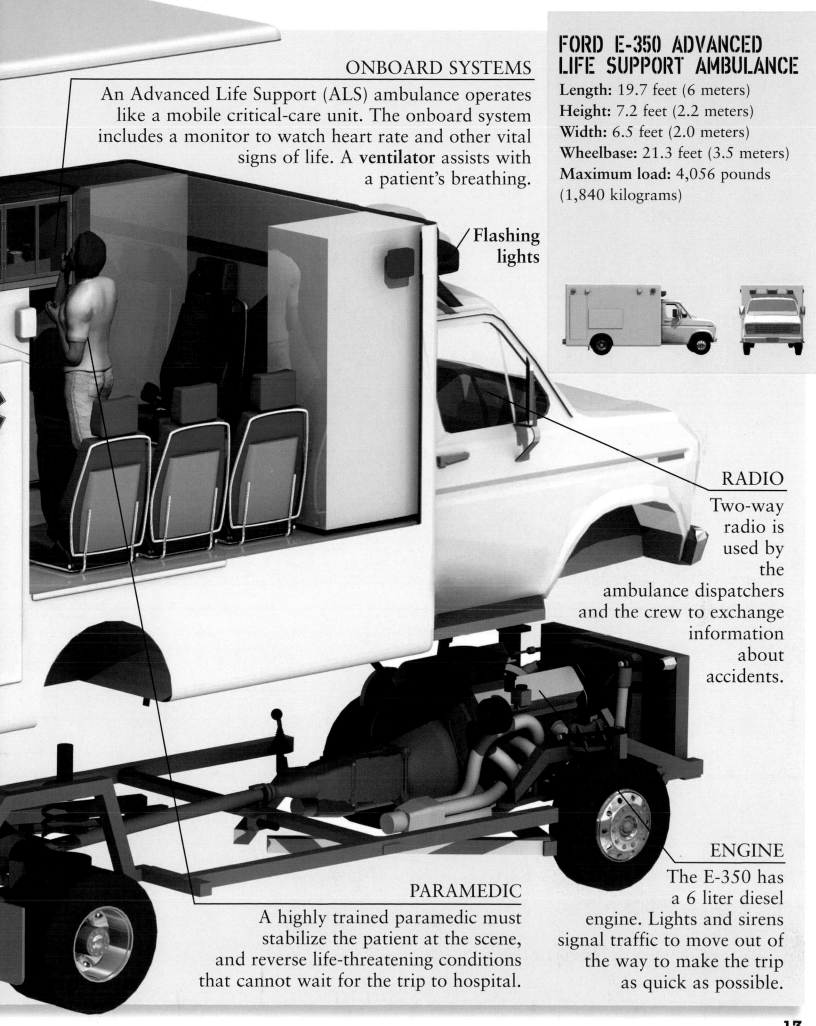

ONBOARD SYSTEMS

An Advanced Life Support (ALS) ambulance operates like a mobile critical-care unit. The onboard system includes a monitor to watch heart rate and other vital signs of life. A **ventilator** assists with a patient's breathing.

Flashing lights

FORD E-350 ADVANCED LIFE SUPPORT AMBULANCE

Length: 19.7 feet (6 meters)
Height: 7.2 feet (2.2 meters)
Width: 6.5 feet (2.0 meters)
Wheelbase: 21.3 feet (3.5 meters)
Maximum load: 4,056 pounds (1,840 kilograms)

RADIO

Two-way radio is used by the ambulance dispatchers and the crew to exchange information about accidents.

PARAMEDIC

A highly trained paramedic must stabilize the patient at the scene, and reverse life-threatening conditions that cannot wait for the trip to hospital.

ENGINE

The E-350 has a 6 liter diesel engine. Lights and sirens signal traffic to move out of the way to make the trip as quick as possible.

FIRE TRUCK

Fire trucks are the most instantly recognizable rescue vehicles. Their red coloring is an international standard, and their flashing lights and sirens make them hard to miss. Most fire trucks carry both ladders and hoses for reaching trapped people, as well as for putting out fires. Their cabs are usually designed to carry several firefighters, as well as all of their equipment.

ENGINE

This needs to be both powerful and reliable—breaking down during an emergency is the last thing a fire crew needs. This LaFrance fire truck has a 6V Detroit diesel engine.

Sirens

FIREFIGHTERS' EQUIPMENT

*Firefighters wear protective clothing to shield them from falling debris and the worst heat of the fire. Breathing apparatus is used when entering burning buildings, as inhaling smoke can be fatal. Other equipment includes handheld tools, such as **pike poles** and axes, for pulling away burning debris and breaking down doors.*

Mask

Fireproof clothing

Breathing apparatus

Oxygen tank

Regulator

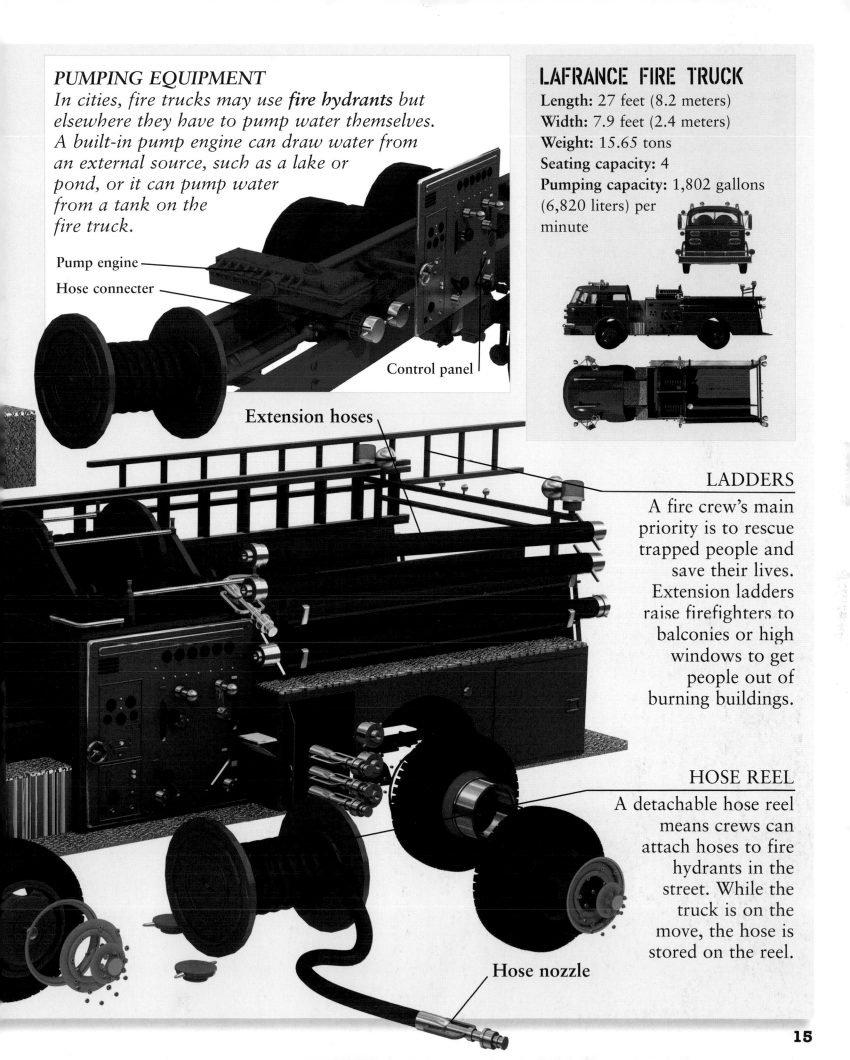

PUMPING EQUIPMENT

*In cities, fire trucks may use **fire hydrants** but elsewhere they have to pump water themselves. A built-in pump engine can draw water from an external source, such as a lake or pond, or it can pump water from a tank on the fire truck.*

Pump engine

Hose connecter

Control panel

Extension hoses

LAFRANCE FIRE TRUCK

Length: 27 feet (8.2 meters)
Width: 7.9 feet (2.4 meters)
Weight: 15.65 tons
Seating capacity: 4
Pumping capacity: 1,802 gallons (6,820 liters) per minute

LADDERS

A fire crew's main priority is to rescue trapped people and save their lives. Extension ladders raise firefighters to balconies or high windows to get people out of burning buildings.

HOSE REEL

A detachable hose reel means crews can attach hoses to fire hydrants in the street. While the truck is on the move, the hose is stored on the reel.

Hose nozzle

AIRPORT FIREFIGHTING VEHICLE

Although, statistically, flying is one of the safest ways to travel, accidents do happen. Airports need to be equipped to deal with accidents. Most large airports have their own firefighting vehicles. These are stationed on-site, usually in a specially designed building with easy access to the runway, in case accidents occur.

FOAM CANNON
This can be pointed in any direction. Its powerful jet allows the vehicle to remain at a safe distance from the fire.

SNOZZLE
Some airport fire trucks carry a snozzle. This is a long boom arm with a sharp end to pierce the aircraft and spray or inject foam inside. It is operated from the cabin by a joystick and aimed with the use of a high-resolution camera. Floodlights help when it is smoky, or at night.

Foam cannon operator

Injector probe

Hardened steel penetrator

Video camera

Floodlight

CREW CABIN
This houses the driver and the foam cannon operator. The large windscreen and side windows give a wide field of view.

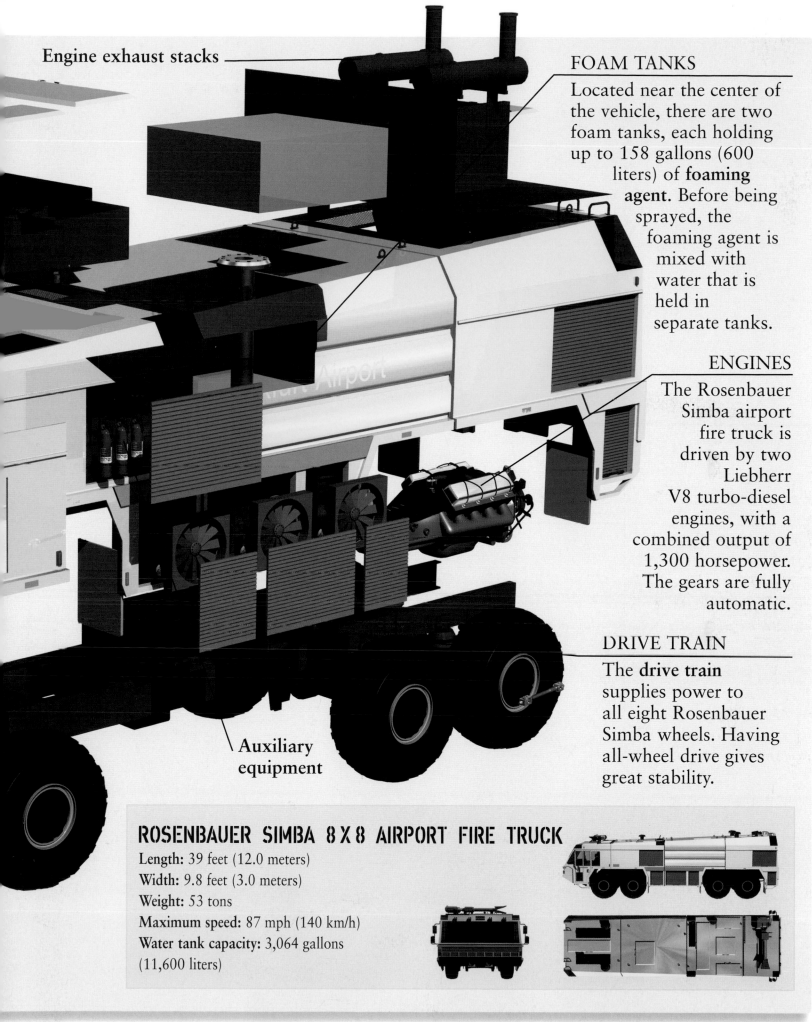

Engine exhaust stacks

FOAM TANKS

Located near the center of the vehicle, there are two foam tanks, each holding up to 158 gallons (600 liters) of **foaming agent**. Before being sprayed, the foaming agent is mixed with water that is held in separate tanks.

ENGINES

The Rosenbauer Simba airport fire truck is driven by two Liebherr V8 turbo-diesel engines, with a combined output of 1,300 horsepower. The gears are fully automatic.

DRIVE TRAIN

The **drive train** supplies power to all eight Rosenbauer Simba wheels. Having all-wheel drive gives great stability.

Auxiliary equipment

ROSENBAUER SIMBA 8 X 8 AIRPORT FIRE TRUCK

Length: 39 feet (12.0 meters)
Width: 9.8 feet (3.0 meters)
Weight: 53 tons
Maximum speed: 87 mph (140 km/h)
Water tank capacity: 3,064 gallons (11,600 liters)

TOW TRUCK

Tow trucks are among the most common rescue vehicles of all. Their job is to rescue people's broken-down vehicles. Most tow trucks are designed to pull light vehicles, such as cars, but a few are more heavy duty. The Mack 60 Ton Wrecker is built to tow other trucks.

EXHAUST STACKS

These pipes transfer exhaust fumes from the huge engine into the air behind the cab.

Sleeper cab

CAB

This is where the driver sits. There is space for a passenger—usually the driver of the broken-down truck—as well as the controls for the truck's equipment.

Horn

Air filter

Radiator

Engine

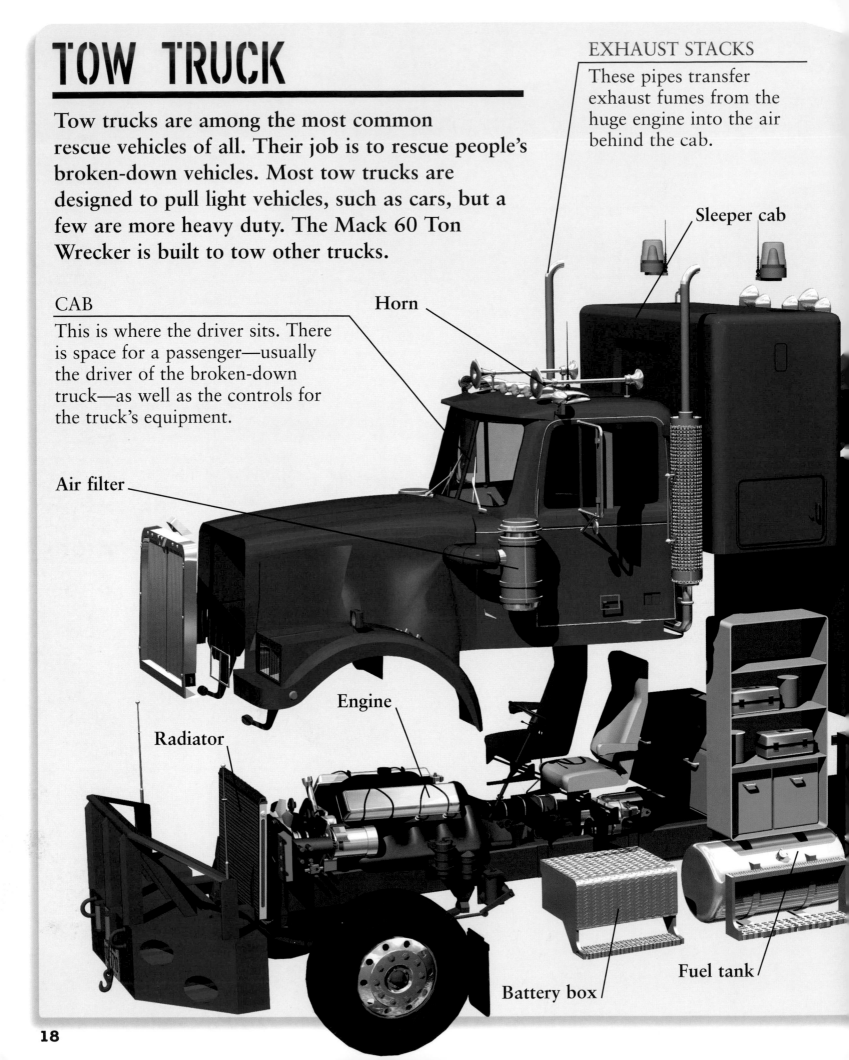

Fuel tank

Battery box

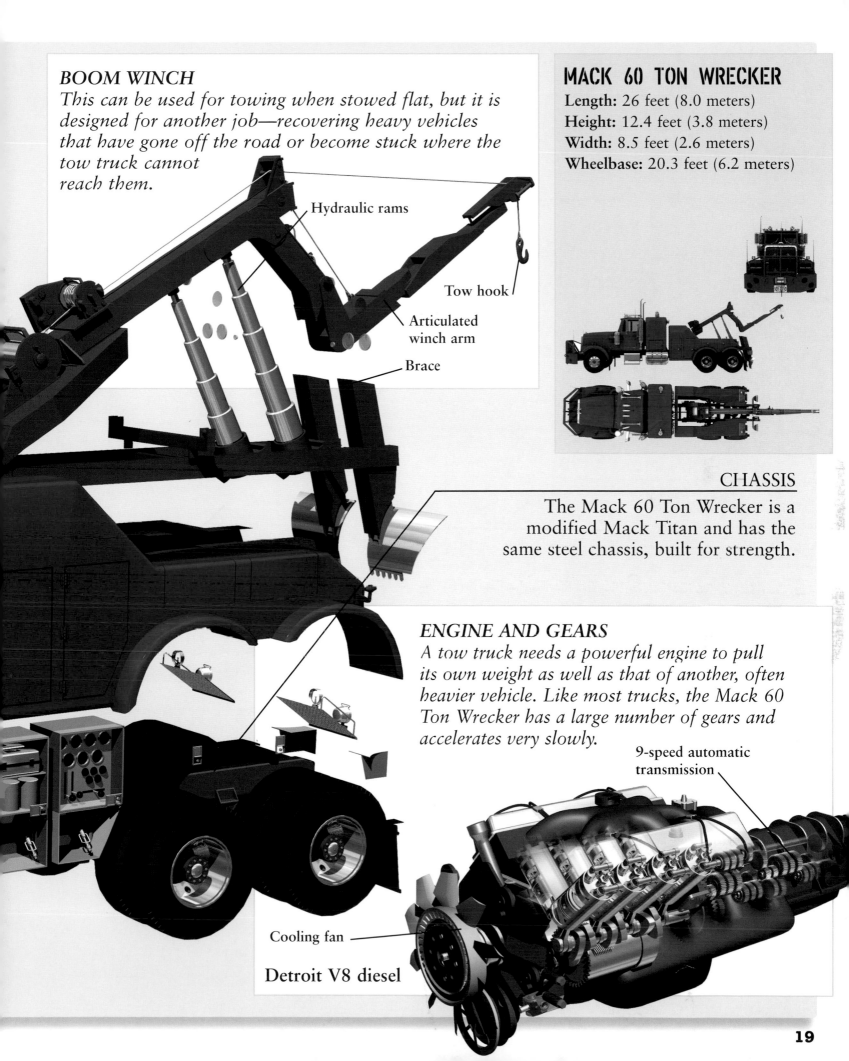

BOOM WINCH
This can be used for towing when stowed flat, but it is designed for another job—recovering heavy vehicles that have gone off the road or become stuck where the tow truck cannot reach them.

Hydraulic rams

Tow hook

Articulated winch arm

Brace

MACK 60 TON WRECKER
Length: 26 feet (8.0 meters)
Height: 12.4 feet (3.8 meters)
Width: 8.5 feet (2.6 meters)
Wheelbase: 20.3 feet (6.2 meters)

CHASSIS
The Mack 60 Ton Wrecker is a modified Mack Titan and has the same steel chassis, built for strength.

ENGINE AND GEARS
A tow truck needs a powerful engine to pull its own weight as well as that of another, often heavier vehicle. Like most trucks, the Mack 60 Ton Wrecker has a large number of gears and accelerates very slowly.

9-speed automatic transmission

Cooling fan

Detroit V8 diesel

SUBMARINE RESCUE VEHICLE (SRV)

There are few places more difficult to perform a rescue than under the sea. Occasionally submarines become entangled and need to be cut loose. If that is not possible then their crews need to be taken back to the surface. This job is undertaken by submarine rescue vehicles like this one.

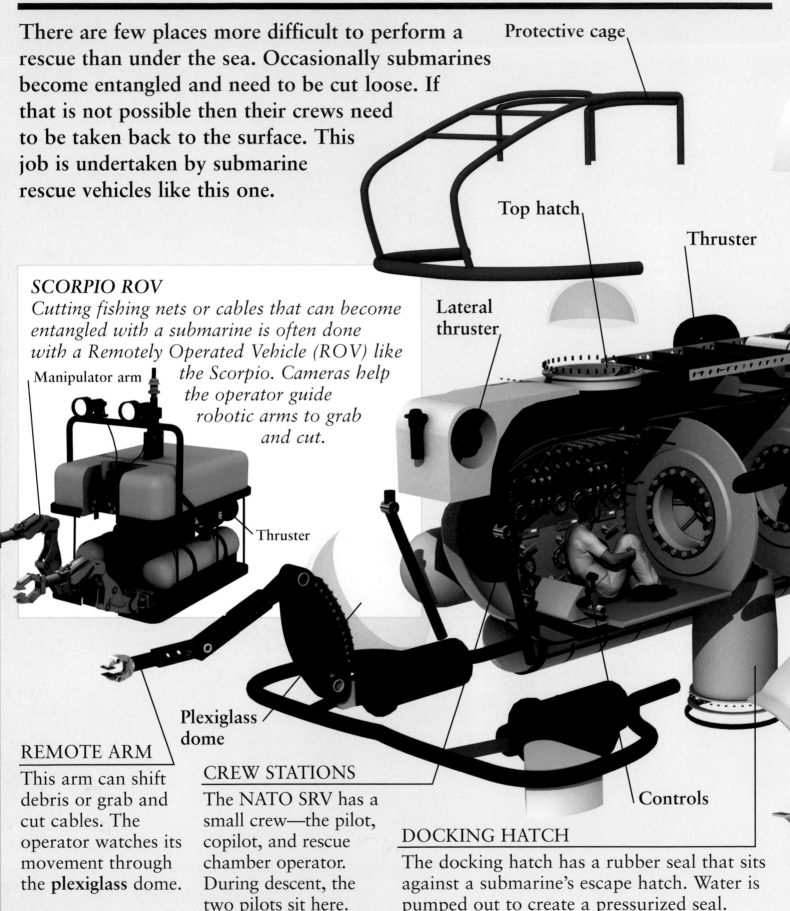

Protective cage

Top hatch

Thruster

Lateral thruster

SCORPIO ROV

Cutting fishing nets or cables that can become entangled with a submarine is often done with a Remotely Operated Vehicle (ROV) like the Scorpio. Cameras help the operator guide robotic arms to grab and cut.

Manipulator arm

Thruster

Plexiglass dome

REMOTE ARM

This arm can shift debris or grab and cut cables. The operator watches its movement through the **plexiglass** dome.

CREW STATIONS

The NATO SRV has a small crew—the pilot, copilot, and rescue chamber operator. During descent, the two pilots sit here.

Controls

DOCKING HATCH

The docking hatch has a rubber seal that sits against a submarine's escape hatch. Water is pumped out to create a pressurized seal.

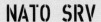

NATO SRV

Length: 32.8 feet (10 meters)
Weight: 29.8 tons
Maximum operating depth: 2,001 feet (610 meters)
Maximum submergence time: 96 hours
Top speed: 4 knots (4.6 mph or 8 km/h)

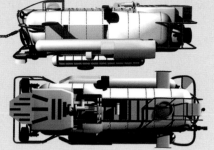

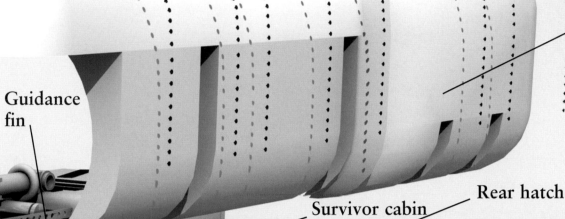

Guidance fin

LIGHT HULL

This "shell" gives the SRV its external shape. Attached to the light hull are the propellers, air tanks, and batteries.

Survivor cabin

Rear hatch

MAIN PROPELLER

There is one propeller on either side of the rear hatch. Each is 23.6 inches (60 centimeters) in diameter.

Motor

Air tank

Battery tank

25 kilowatt electric propeller

Propeller guard

Pressure hull

PRESSURE HULL

The inner hull of the SRV takes all the pressure from the water outside. It is made from a single piece of steel, eliminating the risk of leaks. The cylindrical shape gives it great structural strength. Inside, there is room for fifteen survivors as well as the three-person crew.

LIFEBOAT

Lifeboats are the main vehicles used for rescue at sea. The Tamar class lifeboat is the most advanced vessel in the United Kingdom's RNLI fleet. Introduced in 2005, it uses the computerized Systems and Information Management System (SIMS) that allows the crew to control the lifeboat from the safety of their seats.

SURVIVOR COMPARTMENT

Rescued passengers travel here. Like the rest of the inside of the boat, this room is both watertight and climate-controlled.

BOW THRUSTERS

These enable the boat to move backward. They can also be used with the rear propellers to keep the vessel in position during rescues.

CREW COMPARTMENT

*The Tamar class lifeboat carries a crew of six, including a **coxswain**, a **helmsman**, and an onboard mechanic. Most RNLI crew members are highly trained volunteers. All of the lifeboat's seats have built-in suspension to help smooth the ride in rough seas.*

Crew

Display screen

Safety rail

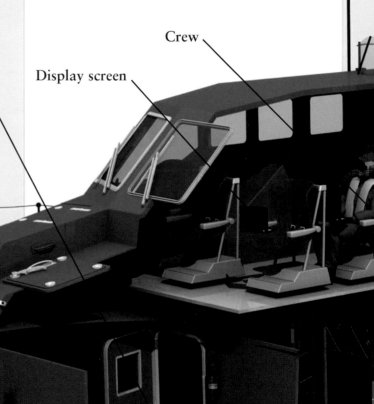

TAMAR CLASS LIFEBOAT

Length: 52.4 feet (16 meters)
Beam: 16.4 feet (5 meters)
Draft: 4.3 feet (1.3 meters)
Top speed: 25 knots (28.8 mph or 46 km/h)
Range without refueling: 286 miles (460 kilometers)

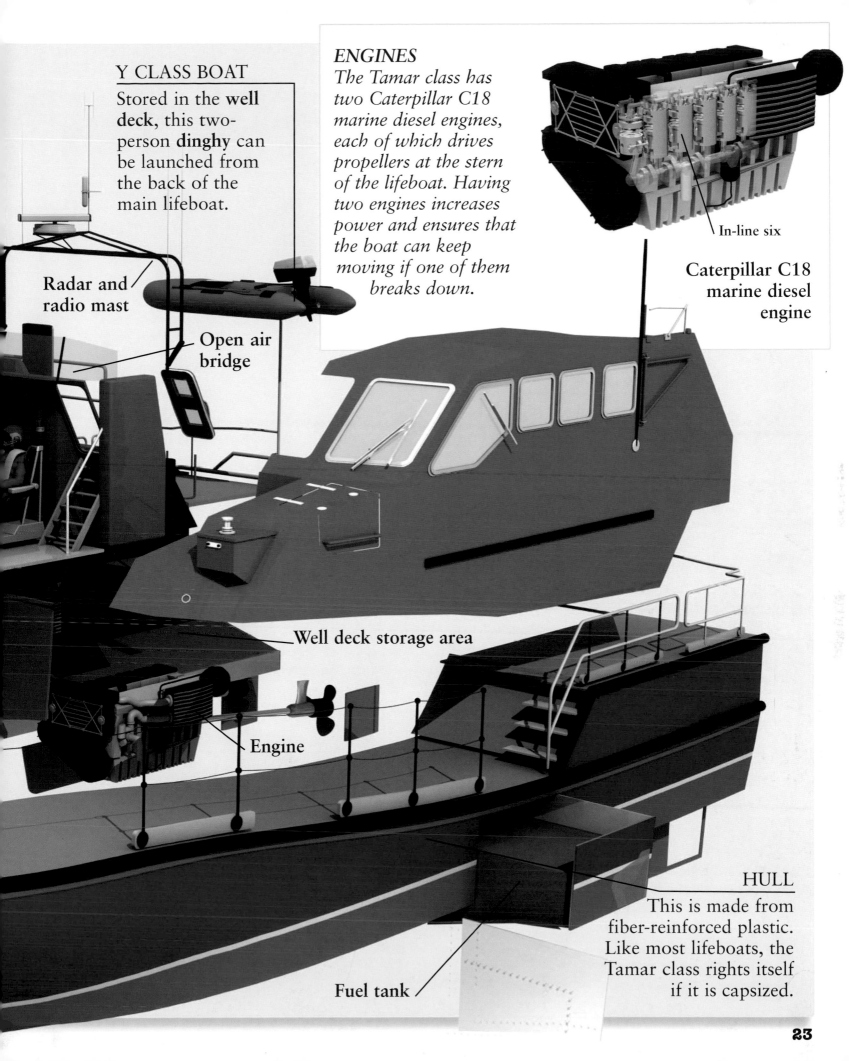

Y CLASS BOAT

Stored in the **well deck**, this two-person **dinghy** can be launched from the back of the main lifeboat.

ENGINES

The Tamar class has two Caterpillar C18 marine diesel engines, each of which drives propellers at the stern of the lifeboat. Having two engines increases power and ensures that the boat can keep moving if one of them breaks down.

In-line six

Caterpillar C18 marine diesel engine

Radar and radio mast

Open air bridge

Well deck storage area

Engine

HULL

This is made from fiber-reinforced plastic. Like most lifeboats, the Tamar class rights itself if it is capsized.

Fuel tank

FIREFIGHTING BOAT

Like all large vehicles, ships are always at risk of catching fire. Many types of boat have been adapted or specially built to act as firefighting vessels, putting out fires on ships in ports or out at sea. Most of these firefighting boats pump the water they use to put out fires from the ocean around them.

Driveshaft from engine

Water feed

Auxiliary pump

Intake pipes

WATER PUMPS
Water is drawn directly from the sea to be sprayed on to the fire. The pumps are normally driven by diesel engines and pressurize the water so that it shoots from the hoses or cannons with enormous force. The powerful jets of water can cross the gaps to burning ships.

NEW YORK CITY FIREBOAT
Length: 128 feet (39 meters)
Width: 31 feet (9.4 meters)
Height: 47.6 feet (14.5 meters)
Weight: 375 tons
Top speed: 14 knots (16 mph or 26 km/h)

FIRE RESCUE

HULL
Most firefighting boats can operate in rough seas if necessary. Often they have deep hulls, like this one.

CRANE

The water cannons used by firefighting boats may be mounted directly on the boats' decks or on top of mobile cranes like this. Cranes have the advantage of height, making it easier to reach burning areas on large ships such as oil tankers.

Water cannon

Operator

Wheel control

RESCUE BOATS

Large firefighting boats carry smaller rescue boats, like this one. These smaller boats can be launched to rescue people who have fallen or jumped into the water to escape the fire.

ENGINES

Firefighting boats vary and so do their engines. One of the largest boats operated by the New York Fire Department is the John D. McKean. It is powered by two 1,000 horsepower direct reversible diesel engines. Two other identical engines drive its water pumps.

Cooling systems

Turbocharger

Oil filters

AIR/SEA RESCUE HELICOPTER

Air/sea rescue helicopters may be used together with, or instead of, lifeboats. They return people to shore more quickly than lifeboats can. Helicopters may also be used to rescue people trapped on cliffs or to airlift them from oil rigs, islands, or isolated beaches. The Westland Sea King is the main rescue helicopter used around the United Kingdom.

Tail rotor

Tail rotor driveshaft

Tailplane

Winch

WESTLAND SEA KING

Rotor diameter: 62 feet (18.9 meters)
Length: 54.7 feet (16.7 meters)
Height: 16.7 feet (5.1 meters)
Top speed: 267 mph (232 km/h)
Range without refueling: 764 miles (1,230 kilometers)

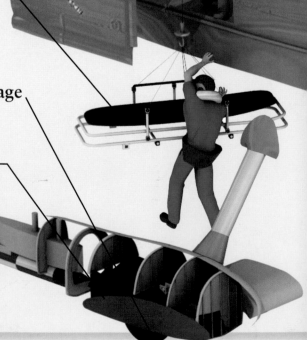

RESCUE CREW

One crew member operates the winch. Another performs the rescue. The winch operator then helps the rescued person to board the helicopter.

Retractable undercarriage

EMERGENCY FLOTATION BAGS

Stowed just above the wheels, these can be inflated rapidly if the helicopter has to land in the sea.

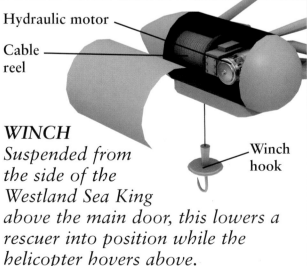

Hydraulic motor

Cable reel

WINCH
Suspended from the side of the Westland Sea King above the main door, this lowers a rescuer into position while the helicopter hovers above.

Winch hook

MAIN BAY

In addition to its four crew members, the Sea King can carry up to six loaded stretchers, or eighteen standing and seated survivors.

ENGINES

The Westland Sea King is powered by two Rolls Royce Gnome engines, positioned just in front of the main rotor blade. A very reliable engine, the Gnome first went into production in 1959.

Rolls Royce Gnome gas turbine

Turbine blades

Exhaust

Intake

Radome

MAIN ROTOR

Designed for shipboard operations, the five main rotor blades can be folded for easy stowage.

FLIGHT CREW

The Westland Sea King is flown by a pilot and a copilot. The largely glass cockpit gives them an excellent field of vision, vital for scanning the water below.

Electronics

FUSELAGE

The Sea King has a metal skinned fuselage. The tail section is hinged so that it can be folded.

Fuel tank

HULL

As well as flotation bags, the Sea King has a boat-shaped hull. This is another safety device to prevent it from sinking, if it crash-lands on water.

AERIAL FIREFIGHTER

Some fires are so large or inaccessible that they can only be dealt with from the air. Known as a "Super-Scooper" or "Duck," the Canadair CL-215 is specially designed to fight such blazes. Introduced into service in 1969, the CL-215 scoops water from lakes during a 12-second, 81 mph (130 km/h) per hour dash over the surface, before returning to the fire with its tanks full.

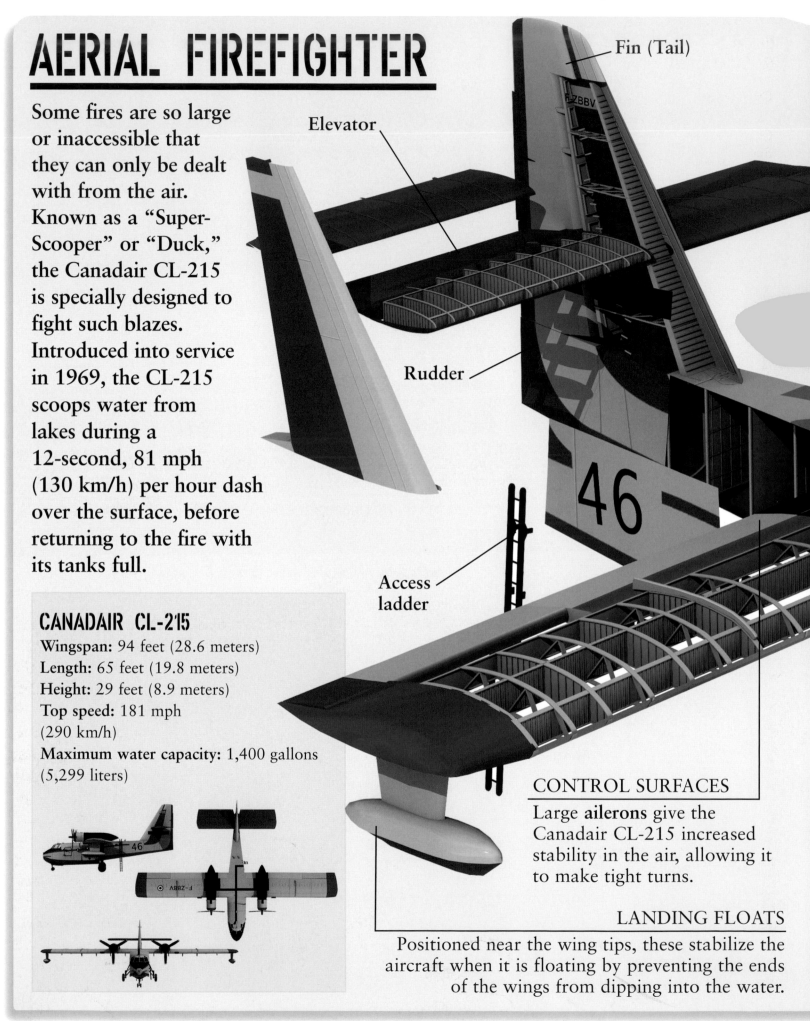

Fin (Tail)

Elevator

Rudder

46

Access ladder

CANADAIR CL-215

Wingspan: 94 feet (28.6 meters)
Length: 65 feet (19.8 meters)
Height: 29 feet (8.9 meters)
Top speed: 181 mph (290 km/h)
Maximum water capacity: 1,400 gallons (5,299 liters)

CONTROL SURFACES

Large **ailerons** give the Canadair CL-215 increased stability in the air, allowing it to make tight turns.

LANDING FLOATS

Positioned near the wing tips, these stabilize the aircraft when it is floating by preventing the ends of the wings from dipping into the water.

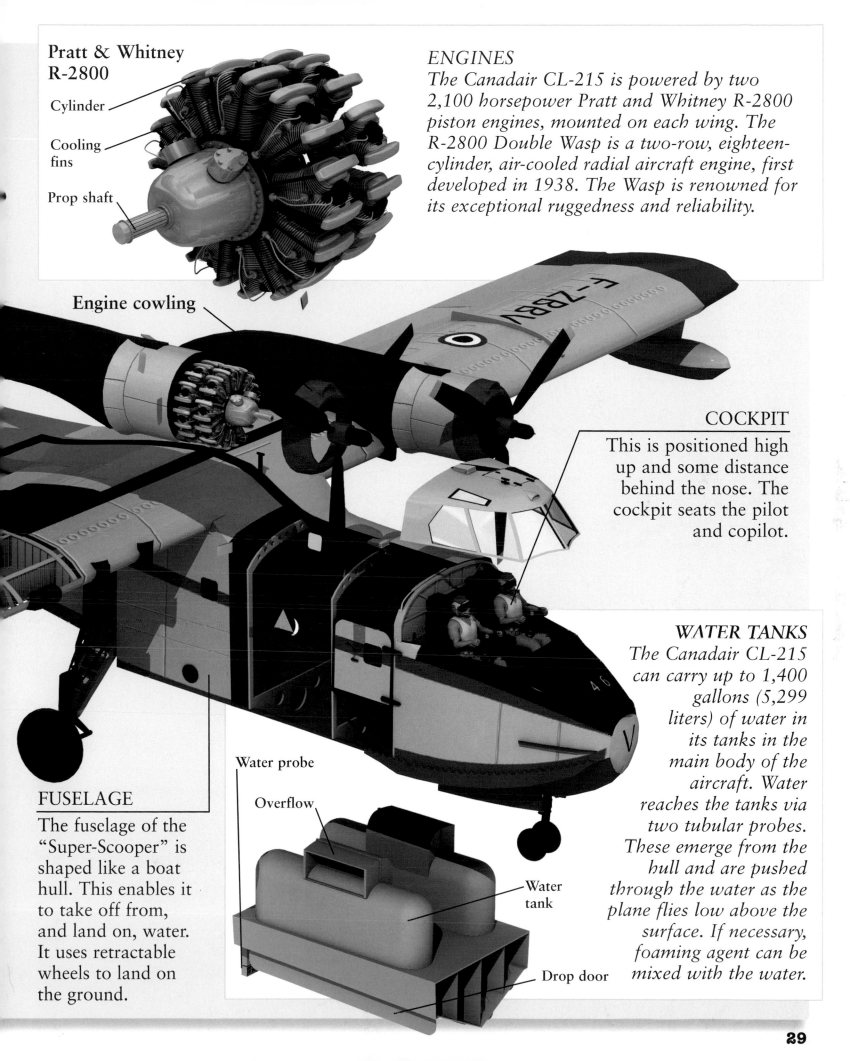

Pratt & Whitney R-2800

Cylinder

Cooling fins

Prop shaft

ENGINES

The Canadair CL-215 is powered by two 2,100 horsepower Pratt and Whitney R-2800 piston engines, mounted on each wing. The R-2800 Double Wasp is a two-row, eighteen-cylinder, air-cooled radial aircraft engine, first developed in 1938. The Wasp is renowned for its exceptional ruggedness and reliability.

Engine cowling

COCKPIT

This is positioned high up and some distance behind the nose. The cockpit seats the pilot and copilot.

WATER TANKS

The Canadair CL-215 can carry up to 1,400 gallons (5,299 liters) of water in its tanks in the main body of the aircraft. Water reaches the tanks via two tubular probes. These emerge from the hull and are pushed through the water as the plane flies low above the surface. If necessary, foaming agent can be mixed with the water.

Water probe

Overflow

Water tank

Drop door

FUSELAGE

The fuselage of the "Super-Scooper" is shaped like a boat hull. This enables it to take off from, and land on, water. It uses retractable wheels to land on the ground.

FUTURE MACHINES

Many of the rescue services will turn to robotic vehicles in the future. Robots are already used in firefighting and rescue operations. They can identify whether certain areas are close to collapse and too dangerous for human teams to enter.

ROSENBAUER PANTHER
Sturdy yet lightweight, the latest airport firefighting vehicle is designed for speed and maneuverability.

One advance in firefighting is the Marsupial Robot, which consists of two robots: one supplies electricity while the other investigates dangerous areas with a video camera and transmits pictures back to the supply robot. Ambulances of the future may have cameras fitted inside and outside to help avoid collisions or a device to change red traffic lights to green. A "shell" concept proposes a removable shell that slides off the ambulance and creates a temporary treatment place.

VUAV "EAGLE EYE"
This Vertical Unmanned Aerial Vehicle is designed to be a U.S. Coast Guard scout and is launched from the deck of a ship.

CARBON MOTORS E7
Due to enter service in 2012, this U.S. vehicle is the first to be built specifically as a police car. Its many features include built-in lights and sirens, and a cockpit with fully integrated factory-fitted law enforcement equipment.

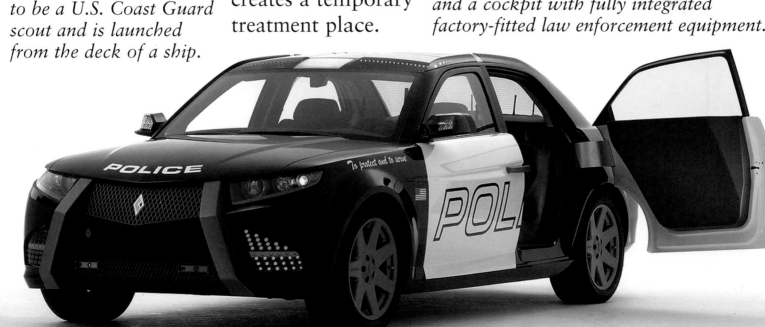

GLOSSARY

ailerons
Hinged control sections on the aircraft wing that are used to help an aircraft turn.

coxswain
The person in charge of a lifeboat's crew. The coxswain may also steer the boat if the helmsman is unable to.

defibrillator
An electrical device used to counteract irregular and rapid heartbeat and restore heartbeat to normal by applying a brief electric shock.

diesel
A type of fuel used by motor vehicles. Diesel is normally oil-based but may also be derived from plant material or other organic matter.

dinghy
A small, open-decked boat.

drive train
The series of moving parts between the engine and the wheels that supplies power to make the wheels turn.

fire hydrant
An upright pipe with a nozzle for drawing water from an underground water supply in an emergency.

foaming agent
A substance that is mixed with water to create a thick foam.

Global Positioning System (GPS)
A system of satellites that allows people with specialized receivers to pinpoint exactly where they are on the Earth.

helmsman
The person who steers a boat or ship.

internal combustion engine
An engine that burns fuels such as gas inside cylinders to generate power.

municipal ambulances
Ambulances that are based in towns or cities and used to transport members of the general public.

pike pole
A long-handled instrument used by firefighters to pull away burning debris when tackling a fire.

plexiglass
An extremely tough transparent plastic used as a substitute for glass.

propeller
A device with twisted blades that forces, or propels, vehicles such as some airplanes and boats, into motion.

radome
A weatherproof cover that protects a radar antenna.

ventilator
A device that supplies oxygen or a mixture of oxygen and carbon dioxide for breathing, particularly to a person who is unable to breathe unaided.

well deck
A deck of a ship that is located at the level of the waterline.

INDEX